UX Design Interviews

The job guide for passing interviews and getting UX Design jobs

Duane Harrison

CONTENTS

INTRODUCTION *4*

PART 1: DESIGN AN OUTSTANDING CV *6*

Gather useful information *6*

Write an effective CV *10*

Tailor-make for UX or UI *13*

CV Sample *18*

PART 2: HAVE A WINNING PORTFOLIO *20*

FAQ for creating a portfolio *20*

Things you need to bear in mind *23*

PART 3: CREATE A GREAT INTERVIEW EXPERIENCE *25*

General Preparation *25*

Prepare to answer interview questions *29*

Introductions *31*

Design process & project experience *35*

Problem-solving *44*

Management skills *48*

Personality & Future Development *56*

Design insight *64*

Employment details *71*

CONCLUSION *74*

INTRODUCTION

Businesses begin to recognise the power of providing good user experience to their customers. They are more willing to hire some UX and UI designers to address their challenges. It means there are lots of opportunities for us to grab. And this is the complete guide to help you do so.

Let me introduce myself. I am Duane Harrison. I joined one of the world's largest banks as a UX Lead in 2018, built and led the team through various product launches. Before that, I worked at one of the world's leading airlines, overseeing the design of their digital experience, as well as working in London at two map related startups.

It has been a journey of travelling, countless internships and interviews, and meeting people from diverse backgrounds. I am thankful for the journey and motivated to share my notes from all these successes and failures. This book is an amalgamation of that.

I have written this book to be practical. We start with writing an outstanding CV and some general tips to perform well at the interview. Then we dig deeper, preparing for the UX design job interview. After that, we will centre around how to answer interview questions, with concrete examples and suggestions included.

The content of this book was elaborated from my notes that got me into different UX internships and companies. I hope you will find it helpful in getting ready to apply for your job.

PART 1: DESIGN AN OUTSTANDING CV

There is research pointing out that your CV approximately has only six seconds to make an impression. You don't like the odds, but your recruiters can be very, very busy. So let's make sure we design a CV that works.

Gather useful information

Start with a skeleton

You may be overwhelmed by the idea of creating a perfect CV in the first place. Don't be. Perfectionism kills productivity. Let's start with a skeleton and focus on choosing useful content. There are a few things you must cover:

Personal Information:

- Name
- Email
- Phone number

Work Experience:

- Name of the company
- Title of the position
- Month and year you worked at the company
- Bullet points describing your duty and achievements

Tips:
- If you have enough working experience, exclude those irrelevant to the job you are applying for.
- Include the city (and country) of the company if you worked abroad.
- Don't exclude unpaid work experience or extracurriculars if they show relevant skills.

Education:

- Name of the institution
- The degree you earn and in what field
- Date of award
- Degree Classification (Optional)

Tips:
- If you went to university, no one cares where you went to high school.
- Include the city (and country if you studied abroad) of the institution if you studied abroad.

Sample Structure of a CV

Name

Contact

Work Experience

Name of Employer - Position / Role	Start Date - End Date
Scope of Duties	

Professional Qualifications

Professional Body	Date of Award & Expiration Date
Qualification Obtained	

Education

Institution	Start Date & Date of Award
Programme & Education Level	

Be selective

A common problem I see is people try to dump everything in their CV. Remember, a CV is a document that convinces the recruiters that you are the most suitable candidate. Therefore, avoid irrelevant job experience, hobbies and interest unless they are professional in content and relevant to the job.

Write an effective CV

Achievements over duties

Filling most of the above information is easy, but your recruiters need more than some plain descriptions. Many people make the mistake of copying their previous position job duties from the web as if they were working experience. Those words tell nothing about your skills.

To make the sections valuable, summarise the job duty with 1-2 sentences. Then highlight your achievements. And it will be way more useful if you can provide statistics to support those statements.

Avoid stupid mistakes

Typos

It sounds impossible to make such a mistake, but typos do

happen. Our minds can trick us into overlooking misspelt words. Just review your CV carefully, and if you can, never send the application in a hurry.

Use the same CV for every application

Even if you have been applying for jobs in the same industry, don't just use the same CV. Create and continue to update a "CV pack" with all the useful information. Use it as a framework to customise a compelling CV that targets the job requirements and description.

Include skills that are too common

Everyone claims to possess interpersonal skills and be a team player. You cannot convince the recruiters by just claiming it. Doing so may give the impression that you don't have other experiences and hard skills worth mentioning instead of an ambiguous claim.

Therefore it is better to avoid general competencies and soft skills that every position needs:

- Interpersonal skills
- Fast learning
- Self-motivated
- Management skills

You should include hard skills, for example:

- The software you can use

- Code you can write

- The language you can speak, etc.

Tips:
- Instead, you can write about your soft skills wisely (page 16) and show them during the interview (page 29) as well.

TLDR

Too Long Didn't Read. Keep it 1-2 pages. Your recruiter is going to scan over the CV. Make sure you don't overwhelm the user. If you want to provide more information, try to build a personal website or an online portfolio or additional fact sheet, then include the link on the CV.

Choosing a horrible filename

Many applicants upload or send their CV without checking the file name. There are "CV.pdf" and "CV(4).pdf". It tells more of your carelessness than the endeavours to amend the CV four times. Name it by your first and last name.

Tailor-make for UX or UI

You're not a robot

No matter how experienced and talented you are, your CV is going to look similar to others at first glance. A short, personalised profile will help. Use it wisely to show your passion for UX design.

Involve UX specific keywords

Please read the job description you're applying for, select the keywords that relate to you, and use them throughout the CV. Here are some examples for our industry:

UX Research
- User research
- Usability test

UX Design
- Experience architecture (Information/Interaction design /Experience design)
- Storyboards
- Mockup
- Wireframe
- Optimisations
- Prototype
- Data

UI Design
- Style Guide

- Design system
- Web Accessibility
- Graphics

Marketing
- Brand-led experiences
- Illustration

Ways of working
- Digital Standards
- Agile
- Scrum

Other / Skills
- iOS
- Android
- Web platform
- Responsive

Show your problem-solving skills

Your potential employer needs to know whether you are a good UX designer who can deal with pain points. Give some details about the problem you solved in the work experience section. These terms will help:

- Improved design / solution design
- Redesign / changes
- Optimisation
- Report issues

Present your soft skills wisely

Okay, I did say avoid those common soft skills in the previous part. So how to reveal your soft skills without making it sound like you're blowing your own trumpet? Like many other things, prove them.

Back up your claims by putting it in context. For example, if you were the team leader in the previous job, write a little about building a team or solving problems. If you would like to show your interpersonal skills, write a little about your collaboration.

Don't over-design it

As a UX designer, you may want to display your creativity and design skills. While you can add a few design elements, a good CV doesn't require your engaging, interactive, and visual works. Save them for your portfolio.

Instead of designing graphics or icons for your CV, you should consider the colour, whitespace, typeface, line length, and breaks. Make sure it is easy to read.

Build your portfolio

To further demonstrate and present evidence of your capabilities, build a portfolio. After all, it is a more visual and definite proof of your capabilities. To help you land your dream job, I will talk about this more in Part 2.

Online presence matters

As mentioned before, a personal website and other online presence can act as some additional information to your recruiters. Some companies will do an online presence search on their potential employees to make sure they are hiring the right person as well. Therefore it is a good idea for you to "search yourself" too.

Take online presence as a dynamic, updated, and findable CV or even portfolio. It can also be a tool for networking and establishing a personal brand. Using social platforms correctly can help you establish an online presence too. Try to build a professional profile on these platforms:

- LinkedIn
- Facebook
- Twitter
- Meetup.com
- Eventbrite
- Quora
- Online course platforms

It is a good idea to network through social media. You can connect with industry professionals, engage in some discussions, and even create some content. To go further, you can attend events and meetups from platforms like meetup.com and

Eventbrite.

When you have doubts, ask questions on Quora or in a related Facebook group. Investing in an online course is an option too.

CV Sample

Edmond Halley

Personalised profile

edmond@ehalley.com
+1-201-258-5720

Personal infomation

Leader in creating great experiences. Passionate about improving practice and process with a focus on customer and data driven design.

EXPERIENCE

Show your problem solving & soft skills

Bank of America, New York, US - UX Lead

Aug 2018 - Present

Built up and managed the Bank of America design team which supports the customer and business products.

- **Design team** Made crucial hires to build up a team of 8 designers. Improved design culture by working closely with UI Lead to raise the profile of design within the organisation. Improved internal design process and workflows.

- **Product** Worked on both customer and merchant sides by delivering the redesign of the Bank of America app and the release of Bank of America Business App.

- **Customer and data driven design** Carried out user research with merchants using various methodologies. Worked on optimisations which improved the signup rate for the Business App.

United Airlines, Chicago, US - Assistant Manager, Experience

Aug 2016 - Aug 2018

Accountable for the design and standards of all user facing digital experiences.

- **Team and management** Responsible for designers on my team and guiding designers under IT department as well as external vendors. Took on role as Product Owner for the Web Accessibility project across the website.

- **Digital Experience** Established Digital Standards and Style Guide ensuring consistent, brand-led experiences. Closely worked with business units and vendors on projects: website, booking flow, online magazine, check-in kiosk and more.

- **Customer focus and data** Work on optimisations that resulted in savings of 1 million USD p.a. Nominated as customer champion within the company and made several impactful customer focused changes.

Provide statistics to show achievement

Q Mapping, New York, US - Senior UX Designer

Oct 2015 - Aug 2016

Worked closely with product manager to validate and deliver SaaS products across all platforms.

- **Mobile and Web app** - Responsible for iOS (iPhone/iPad), Android and Web platform. Worked in agile product delivery by splitting design into releases and flows. Prototyped mobile app interactions before developing and worked closely with engineers to refine build.

- **User research and product delivery** - Joined field studies and interviews with lorry drivers. Worked with user researcher to ensure web product/software met users needs. Focused on delivery by working with PM to manage deadlines, prioritise work and make sure requirements were met.

Involve UX specific keywords

Present your soft skills wisely

Transit, Montreal, Canada - Mobile Designer
Jul 2014 - Oct 2015

Handled a wide range of tasks from working on the design of the app to asset handling, website, emails and user testing.

- **Mobile app** Worked side-by-side with developers to deliver new features and releases on iOS and Android. Improved information architecture by making it easier to understand data on small screens.

- **User testing and QA** Conducted user testing sessions and shared findings to teams. Developed testing plan which helped employees test and report issues. Involved with customer operations by responding to app issues and identified and documented issues.

- **Localisation** Engaged with local users to improve the app experience through copy and optimisation. Introduced asset templates for new markets.

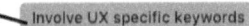 Involve UX specific keywords

Toshiba, Tokyo, Japan - Design Research Intern
Jul 2013 - Sep 2013

Assisted the Product and Service Design team projects working on wireframes, storyboards and field research in Japan.

Google, Mountain View, US - Graphic Design Intern
Jun 2011 - Oct 2011

Produced user flows and wireframes for Google's internal learning application.

Include extracurriculars if they show relevant skills

EDUCATION

California College of the Arts, US
2009 - 2014

BFA Interaction Design

Keio University, Japan
2011 - 2012

Design Management (exchange), Awarded scholarship

PART 2: HAVE A WINNING PORTFOLIO

A portfolio is critical to UX and UI designers, so I assume you do have one. If you don't, this section will help you start building one. Be reminded that to create a winning portfolio requires a lot of technique and even a marketing mindset, which requires more than a chapter to discuss. Therefore, you may take this chapter as a checklist to brush up your portfolio or a starter kit.

FAQ for creating a portfolio

What to put in?

I recommend picking your best three or five projects, depending on the breadth and depth you want to show.

Which projects should I choose?

Projects which are the most successful and impactful. More importantly, those that are related to the roles you are applying for. For example, if you are applying for a mobile UX designer role, ideally your portfolio should include two out of three mobile-related projects. Furthermore, pick the ones that you are most passionate about and that you know inside out.

What to do if I don't have any (or relevant) projects?

Create them. Seriously, it's worth your time. A self-made UX project will definitely be more valuable than irrelevant work.

Tips:
- I used to go to tech meetups, looking for willing developers to cooperate on side projects. Designers and developers can complement each other's skills. Besides, it is an excellent way to expand your network.

What to say about the projects?

Focus on story and content. You can use the SCAR Framework. Explain your work as you are telling a good story, talk about the Situation, Challenge, Action and Results. Here is an example of how you should structure it.

Project Title
Your Role
Year/duration
Project type

Situation: Context about the case. For example, what company, or which departments are involved etc.

Challenge: What problem were you trying to solve?

Actions: Describe the methodologies and processes. How do you find the solution?

Result: What are the positive changes? Try to quantify your achievement, for instance, how much cost/time your work saves?

Extra kick: Talk about what you have learned, show that you know how to extract experience and knowledge from your works. It means you possess soft skills like strategic thinking and self-awareness.

What is the best format for Portfolio?

PDFs are becoming outdated; websites are preferred. It allows you to update frequently and add your own design elements. More importantly, it can be interactive. So be creative. At one point I coded my own portfolio and included the functionality of tooltips which displayed extra information on certain parts of my work. The viewer could dig in deeper about specific aspects, and the whole portfolio was a bit more engaging. Little touches can make sure your portfolio stands out.

When to stop?

Never! I mean, an artist never stops, right? Always update it. For example, as you gain more work experience, you will have more sophisticated and independent projects to share. By then, you need to replace the older ones from your younger self! By keeping updating the portfolio, it will allow you to have more case studies in hand, which will help create a tailor-made portfolio when needed.

Things you need to bear in mind

Presentation matters

Remember to present your projects well, don't neglect the corresponding copy with it. Make sure it looks tidy and readable on various devices. The visuals should be top quality in case the viewer uses a large screen to read it.

Pursue progress, not perfection

Creating a winning portfolio can be stressful. It can take a long time, you need to break the perfection dilemma. Stop using "my portfolio isn't good enough or isn't ready" as an excuse. This guide encourages you to apply for interviews and jobs constantly, and the portfolio you bring along should be continuously improved too.

Treat it like a product, with a version 1 and a version 2 and so on while making the vital improvements early. Did you know the first iPod only had 240 songs? Experience and attempts really go far, and you'll learn far more by doing this, rather than telling yourself you will only apply when your portfolio is 'finished.'

PART 3: CREATE A GREAT INTERVIEW EXPERIENCE

For many, a job interview is a final challenge between you and the job you want. Let us do this right.

General Preparation

Know your User

Knowing your users is one of the fundamental design rules. Now, try to see the interview as a product. The users (recruiters) use it to find someone capable of hiring instead of giving you a hard time. They also look for someone they want to work with, a potential teammate. So get over your fear and concentrate on creating a satisfying interview experience.

You are the interviewer, too

The most fundamental and vital advice is to walk in the room with the mindset of a two-way interview. The interview is a conversation between you and the hiring department. You are there to see whether to be on board. With this in mind, you'll be more confident.

Be confident, but not overconfident

You are amazing. Still, make sure you will achieve the best version of yourself. Preplan everything so even small details are covered.

- Research the company
- Prepare the answer to the interview questions
- Practice your answer
- Make an interview kit
    - Extra copies of your CV
    - Information on at least one referee
    - A notebook & pen
    - Portfolio
- Plot out your route
- Get enough sleep
- Dress the right way
- Arrive Early

Tips:
- I used to write down all the questions and answers in a Google Doc. I would go for walks in the day or night, and then I would ask myself those questions and rehearse the answers until I could remember it off by heart.
- If your portfolio requires the internet, make sure you are prepared either beforehand or tether to your phone. You should prepare an offline version in case there are any connection problems.
- Set your arrival time in the Citymapper app to plan your route. You never know what might go wrong on the day.

Extra tips for a telephone interview

A phone interview requires a slightly different kind of preparation. Here are my tips:

- Research the company

- Prepare answers to the interview questions

- Practice your answer

- Make an interview kit

  - A copy of your CV

  - Information on at least one referee

  - A notebook & pen

  - Portfolio

- Print out your prepared materials, including:

  - Questions and answers (you can tailor-make a

cheat sheet from this guide!)

- CV
- Cover letter
- Critical information about the company
- Practice (just because you got all your notes in hand doesn't mean you can skip the practice)

- Get enough sleep
- Dress the right way
  - You don't need to dress up, but you should not wear your pyjamas too. Clothes affect your attitude, and more importantly, your confidence.

- Prepare a pleasant environment
  - Make sure you have enough surface area for all your notes.
  - Have a notepad and pen just in case you need to write something down.
  - Prepare a glass of water. You may not need it but prepare for the worst such as a sudden tickle in your throat.

- Relax
  - Without the commute, you will have more time to prepare yourself before the interview. Have a good breakfast, drink coffee, go to the gym or whatever that gets you in the routine and feel

confident.

- Wear earphones if you want (earphones can help you listen more clearly and leaves your hands free for taking notes or natural body language)
- To be more natural, wait for two rings first, then answer the call.

Prepare to answer interview questions

Countless unknown variables are waiting to throw you off during the interview. Though, preparing your answer will always help. When you interview for an UX/ UI design job, you will probably come across the following types of questions:

- Introduction
- Design process and project experience
- Ways of working
    - Problem-solving
    - Management skills
    - Personality & Future development
    - Design insight
- Employment details

The companies mentioned onwards are just used as examples,

however the situations given can be very real. We will walk through them one by one. But beforehand, there are few basic and significant techniques we need to bear in mind.

Remember the purpose and show off your soft skills

Soft skills are difficult to demonstrate in your own words. Hence, an interview is not an everyday conversation but a valuable opportunity to promote yourself. Take a second to organise the answer for each question, make sure you are clear, calm and stick to the point.

SCAR format, Situation, Challenge, Actions and Results

All recruiters want to evaluate your problem-solving skills. I usually answer those questions in SCAR format. It can ensure you provide enough details and emphasise the resolutions and result. You will then look well-prepared and knowledgeable about your experience.

Prove what you say

This point is more like an elaboration from the above two. Always provide a solid example, tell short stories so that your answer will be convincing. Whenever possible, quantify your achievement.

Introductions

These are the questions often asked at the beginning of the interview. It is your big chance to make a great first impression.

Q1. Tell me about yourself? / Walk me through your background?

Aim of the question: Yes, the recruiters received your CV. Yet they will always ask you to introduce yourself to know about you as well as your presentation skills.

Strategy:

✓ Summarise your primary selling points (professional background, strengths) to prove that you are the one they should invest in.

✓ Show your personality.

✗ Going too granular on the details.

✗ Simply repeat your CV content.

✗ Sounding negative and desperately needing a job.

✓ **Example**

I am currently the UX Lead in the digital team at the Bank of America. I was the Assistant Manager for Digital Experience at United Airlines, overseeing Digital Experience. Before that, I worked in London, at two startups, one well known, one not so well known: Transit and Q Mapping.

I'm lucky enough to have been able to have experience in different scale companies in different countries. I enjoy making products with a strong user focus. Although I love my current role, I am ready for some new challenges.

Q2. Tell me about your current role? / Describe your current job responsibilities.

Aim of the question: Know more about your experience and accomplishment related to the responsibilities of the job you apply for.

Strategy:

✓ Connect your responsibilities to the job you apply for.

✓ Talk about the tasks of your current job.

✓ Show that you collaborate with other roles e.g. Product Managers or Developers.

✓ Provide details to show your values e.g. creating wireframes.

✗ Listing job duties.

✗ Describing absolutely everything that you do.

X Describing not much e.g. 'I only create wireframes'.

✓ Example

As a UX lead, I assisted in managing a team of eight designers. I ensured we worked with each owner on different products, including business, customer, APIs, and Portal. I led the UX team to work closely with UI, Copy and Product Management teams. I supported the team to create and review flows or wireframes.

Q3. Why (this role) at (this company)? / What made you interested in applying for this position?

Aim of the question: Confirm that you understand the role and the brand.

Strategy:

✓ Research the position and the company beforehand.

✓ Demonstrate awareness of role and industry, preparedness and passion.

✓ Talk about the positive contributions you could offer.

X No clear reason or just saying you are trying it out.

X Motivated by prestige or the fact the company is a leader, rather than the specific role

X Show little understanding of the company or role.

✓ Example (Lead UX Designer at Goldman Sachs)

I have worked at two startups and an airline. I am devoted to improving every product and adding value. Because there are no longer opportunities for growth that align with my career goals, I am looking for new challenges.

I always want to focus on user-centred design and bring value to it. This role fits perfectly with my skill set and how I'm looking to grow in my career. I am also looking to join a company like Goldman Sachs that designs to change the industry. I noticed that this job would require me to do UX Research, sprint planning and test new products. These are all tasks that entwine with my passion and expertise.

Q4. Why are you looking for new opportunities? / Why did you leave your job?

Aim of the question: To make sure you won't bring any trouble or going to have a short stint that disrupts the company.

Strategy:

✓ Try to be honest but diplomatic.

✓ In most cases you should be looking for a new challenge that you may not have the opportunity to grow in your current role.

✓ Whatever the reason is, start with a positive word about your current/previous position.

✓ Slip in a plug for yourself.

✓ Be self-motivated. Focus on what you are looking for instead of explaining why you left.

✗ Trash talk about your current/previous role.

✗ Bring up money.

✗ Too vague.

✓ Example

I'm actually quite happy at Bank of America but leaving for a new challenge. Bank of America has been a great learning experience for me, hiring a full team, working on two product launches and iterating further. There were many successful projects and changes.

I would love to take these skills to the next level, play a more vital role, which impacts products, strategies and the product road map. I would love the opportunity to work where I can bring customer research and feedback to the table, raise the standards of UX Engineering and work with a global team.

Design process & project experience

To understand whether you are suitable for the position, the recruiters need to understand your design process and project experience. It is a crucial part of the interview. Do you remember I once said there are smarter ways to show your problem-solving skills than merely writing it on the CV? Answering the following questions is one of them. Remember to organise the answer with SCAR technique along the way.

Q1. Describe your design process.

Aim of the question: To understand your thought process and test your knowledge about the job too.

Strategy:

✓ There is no right answer to this question. Describe and explain your process orderly.

✓ A good answer will start with an analysis or research

✓ Explain why you use this approach.

✗ Too vague.

✗ Too open.

✓ **Example** (an outline of ideas for a response)

1. Analyse requirements or problems.
   a. Understand the needs of the business and users
   b. Gain insight from data
2. Plan considering time/scope/quality to figure out the size and scale of the task. Is it for one designer or does it require a collaboration?
3. Conduct User Research, decide on what methodologies to use depending on the problem and resource.
4. Create a wireframe, establishing the basic experience.
5. Perform user tests, evaluating the design in terms of user flow and experience. Look for improvements.
6. Get feedback and alignment.
7. Work on the interface design.
8. Grooming with Developers.

Q2. Describe your UX research methodologies.

Aim of the question: UX designers may favour various research strategies and methods. This question doesn't have a model answer. The recruiters only need to know how you arrange the research tasks.

Strategy:

✓ Explain the reason why you plan your research that particular way.

✓ Cover the advantages of why some methodologies are better than others.

✓ Example

The methodologies I use depend on the type of project. For example, information architecture. I will curate content and create different variations, and ideally, relevant stakeholders should be involved. The research for this kind of project will be more quantitative with many different outcomes.

Usability testing works well for designers to identify the patterns in error and other significant issues in our products. It works well with a small sample size, around several users and testing only a few different variations.

While card sorting is more in-depth and guides the team to understand a user's mental model and specific reasons behind the user's actions.

Q3. Do you have experience working in agile/scrum?

Aim of the question: To know whether you have experience working in agile and see if you can fit in with their ways of working.

Strategy:

✓ Each company will work in agile/scrum differently. Provide an example that shows your knowledge of the skills.

✓ Be honest about your skills, but show that you use them.

✓ Show that you can adapt and mention under what circumstances you will use the corresponding skills.

✓ Example

Yes. Throughout the app development of the Bank of America app, the company adopted the agile approach and worked in sprints.

For each product increment, we execute four sprints which are two weeks long. At the planning session and an alignment event, we mapped out dependencies and did several rounds of prioritisation.

I am not a scrum master but adopt some approaches from it to shield the team from distractions and remove any blockers. Those approaches also helped to build a self-organised team, including carrying out design reviews.

The approach changes according to tasks' needs as well. For example, the team adopted daily stand-ups and Kanban for the projects as well as the hiring process.

Q4. A project you are most proud of and why?

Aim of the question: To understand what motivates and interests you. To know what you would consider as an achievement. The answer may determine whether you are suitable for the company's tasks and overall work culture.

Strategy:

✓ Make sure the example is something you worked hard on and worth being proud of.

✓ Use relevant project examples for the applying job role or company, for instance, use a real app you made as an example to apply for a 'mobile' design job at a start-up.

✓ Include the required details to show how impactful the project is. Be concise about the problem, how you got there, what were the blockers and the result (SCAR technique).

✗ Proud of achieving something through pure luck rather than hard work and professionalism.

✗ Not sounding excited to talk about your best work.

✓ Example (SCAR format)

I am proud of solving problems before and during the launch of the Bank of America Business app.

Situation: The previous team designed Bank of America for Business. When my team took over, I noticed only two out of seven merchants successfully onboarded without asking for help. There must be a problem.

Challenge: When we raised the problem, it was close to the launching day, so we needed to decide whether to go or hold. The company decided to delay the launch.

Action: My team regrouped and analysed the problem. We realised users dropped out of the sign-up process because they usually don't have the required information ready. We proposed to send an email to communicate with our users while designing an in-app checklist that will appear before they start the sign-up process.

Results: In the end, we successfully improved the onboarding flow by 3.5 times, from a high failure rate to a high success rate. I am proud that my team overcame the problem under the tight schedule. Furthermore, getting it all fixed reminded me of how design makes an impact.

Tips:

- Be prepared for some follow-up questions, such as: What would you do differently if you could do the project over? What was your specific contribution to the project?

Q5. *Give an example of a project which gave a lot of impact?*

Aim of the question: To understand how you contribute to a team or company and your ability to manage crucial tasks.

Strategy:

✓ Choose good examples.

✓ Be specific, talk through your process.

✓ Break down responsibilities and explain your part clearly.

✓ **Example**

During my time at United Airlines, I worked across departments and focused on UX optimisations. I led a customer experience task force, gathering all issues from the Global Call Centre and also attending analytics meetings. After analysis from both sources, I successfully identified payment problems and implemented multiple improvements. They prevented the company from 1 million USD weekly loss in revenue, not to mention reduced calls and complaints.

I also revamped and rewrote the error messages. I realised they are too technical for customers. Therefore I worked with the content team to rewrite those messages in a more appropriate tone of voice.

Q6. Give an example of a project where you tackled a customer pain point?

Aim of the question: To know your problem-solving skills.

Strategy:

✓ Use the SCAR technique.

✓ Use examples of collaboration, stakeholders and having a customer focus.

✓ Be specific on how you solve the problem and the outcome.

✗ Complain about the customer or the situation.

✓ **Example**

When I worked at United Airlines, I tackled one of the biggest complaints, which was missing connections. After meeting with the call centre and the Customer Relations Department, I tried different designs and ran A/B tests. Based on the result, I decided to use a more transparent approach and implemented a warning sign showing there will be a short connection time.

My work is holistically aligned with the company strategy and improves connection experience without affecting the revenue. The data retrieved in this project also helped out ground-staffs to assist passengers getting to their connection.

Q7. Tell me about a project that didn't go as planned? / What has been your biggest challenge?

Aim of the question: To know how you behave under pressure or when things are kind of out of hand.

Strategy:

✓ Prove that you possess desirable soft skills, for example problem-solving, collaborative or leadership skills.

✓ Express your belief in continuous improvement.

✗ Elicit empathy instead of focusing on how you overcame the obstacle.

✓ Example

The redesign of the Bank of America app was a 'never-ending' project that was big in scope and had difficult deadlines. There were new features continually added to the app before it was built. As the UX lead, sometimes, it meant leading my team to redesign or adjust it accordingly with a tight deadline.

For example, we released the new feature: Faster Payments System. It was a new and not so well defined feature. To make things worse, people outside of my team were leaving the project and the bank itself. Some problems are well beyond my team's area, causing back and forth with other departments which was time-consuming.

To solve the problem, I work closely with the release team and the product owners to deal with items. My team started daily standups with Business Analysts for unblocking any issues. These measures help to boost efficiency by working on agreements. We were able to deliver the new features on time.

Problem-solving

Q1. Tell me about a time you had to manage conflicting views in your job?

Aim of the question: To assess your communication skills, including your ability to work collaboratively with other disciplines while influencing from a user experience perspective.

Strategy:

✓ Use the SCAR technique.

✓ Demonstrate you took initiative.

✓ Show that you have good communication skills and respect for your colleagues.

✓ Show that you aligned on the problem.

✓ Focus on the user and use of data or research.

✗ No explanation of how the conflict was resolved.

✗ No signs of collaboration.

✗ Escalate before trying to resolve the problem.

✗ Give up or just listen to manager.

✓ Example

In some instances, there would be disagreement between more than one of my superiors and it would lead to an intensive discussion with an unclear direction. There was disagreement about the content for one of the navigation tabs on the Bank of America app.

To resolve this, I organised a workshop about the navigation tab in question with the important stakeholders. I stressed it was necessary to attend and carefully scheduled it so everyone could join. Leading the session, I listened to the different approaches and discussed how it affects the customer. We managed to agree on a solution that was easily possible but true to the original principles of the app.

I made it very clear about which approach we agreed upon with all stakeholders. To avoid any ambiguity, I also sent out a summary of the discussion and what was agreed upon after this session.

Q2. Tell me about a time working with a difficult client/someone you don't get on with?

Aim of the question: To assess your communication skills, including your ability to convince someone and manage a difficult person.

Strategy:

✓ Use the SCAR technique.

✓ Show that you will deal with the conflict in a calm attitude and be able to find resolution independently.

✓ Show that you have good listening and communication skills.

✓ Demonstrate that you are capable of creating a compelling argument. For instance, use customer insight or data to support your views.

✗ No explanation of how the conflict was resolved.

✗ Ignore the client's concerns and follow your own ideas.

✗ Not being respectful. Saying something insulting about a colleague.

✓ Example

There was a product owner who rejected my team's designs and was strong in his own direction. Instead of just going along with some distinct problematic ideas, I decided to convince him professionally. I scheduled a meeting to understand his concerns. Then I directed the discussion based on the data collected from user research so that we can work unbiasedly to explore different approaches. I convinced him using some data I collected about our user journeys, explained what worked and what didn't. By then, I would remind myself to be goal-oriented and make sure to listen to other opinions. In the end, we came up with an agreeable phased approach.

In some cases, some disagreements cannot be resolved. I would speak to other members of the team, such as another manager to get advice or help.

Q3. Any examples of turning a bad situation into a good one?

Aim of the question: To evaluate your problem-solving skill from an actual example and to shed light on whether you have a positive attitude or not.

Strategy:

✓ Use the SCAR technique.

✓ Show resilience and that you always strive to improve

✓ **Example**

There are plenty of examples. Problems are opportunities for UX designers since we always look into problems but take a step back to see what value we can add through design.

For instance, we kept adding new features to the Profile and Settings page to the extent that it got a nickname - the 'mile-long list'. This situation drove us to redesign the page and introduce the 'New' tag. The new Profile and Settings page improved the experience of the Bank of America app massively and offered a more scalable approach to house new features which met business needs.

Management skills

As the interview goes, the recruiters will dig deeper into your working style to evaluate whether you are a team player and be able to fit in the company culture.

Q1. What is your experience managing juniors / a team?

Aim of the question: To see whether you acquire management skills and team spirit.

Strategy:

✓ Emphases management skills and style.

✓ Provide numbers to be more convincing.

✓ Provide a good mix of strategic and managerial experiences.

✓ **Example**

Currently, I am the leader of the Bank of America UX team, leading eight designers with three direct reports. I don't micromanage, but assign work depending on team members' capacity and strengths. I allow them to own the work, come up with solutions on their own.

I am also responsible for removing blockers, arranging the grooming with the developers. I work closely with UI, Copy, and Business Analysts, arrange weekly meetings and small catch-ups to ensure our work aligned with the company's goals and the key performance indicators. Moreover, I organise customer research and teach the benefits of it.

Outside the team, I am managing conflicts between groups indirectly. I will first understand the problem, then provide resources, work-force, and technical support. Sometimes, I cannot resolve the tension, yet I can provide customer feedback or data and guide us towards the solutions.

Tips:

- Even if you are in a junior or senior role, you can still be a bridge between other disciplines (e.g. between the developers and Product Managers) and you can still manage stakeholders or other teams (e.g. a spreadsheet to track project progress or goals with other teams).

Q2. What is your experience of leadership?

Aim of the question: To know how well you can lead a team to get things done, especially if you are applying for a management role.

Strategy:

✓ Include several aspects of leadership in your answer

✓ Show that you are capable of achieving your own goals as well as the company's goals

---

✓ Example

As the UX team leader of the Bank of America app, I used my communication and presentation skills to introduce ideas at an all hands company meeting. I was also responsible for running in sprints, helping prioritise features. I also led the day to day running, supporting over three designers in my team to ensure our projects were completed.

More importantly, I brought the profile of the design Team up. I fought for the team and therefore we had a seat at the table as early as in road mapping sessions of the app. I succeeded in this mission as the team I led is now seen to be a creative partner in the development process.

Tips:

- Even if you don't have experience as a manager, reference examples where you have taken initiative without help from superiors.

Q3. *What is your experience in product management?*

Aim of the question: To know more specifically about your working experience.

Strategy:

✓ Include several aspects of product leadership in your answer.

✓ Start with the bigger picture and then also include the smaller details.

✓ Show that you are capable of achieving the company's goals.

✓ Example

When I was working at United Airlines, in addition to the day to day management of my team, I also managed vendors; successfully overseeing the UX design process on various projects, including the fares website, the inflight wifi portal and the booking engine.

As a Product Owner for Web Accessibility, I also led a scrum team to deliver business needs and prioritise resources to align with the brand values and the users' interests. This included ensuring the product's features launched according to schedule, planning sprints and allocating work based on teammates' skills and capacity.

Even after this, I was an active member of the Web Accessibility Champion team, ensuring accessibility continued to be a priority and requirement at United Airlines.

Q4. What is your experience managing under-performers?

Aim of the question: To understand what you define as problematic behaviour and the standard of performance.

Strategy:

✓ Show that you would align and understand the situation.

✓ Emphasise how your management style would help an employee's performance.

✓ Give practical and sensible suggestions.

✗ Bad-mouthing the employee.

✗ Avoid debatable performance, such as being opinionated.

✓ Example

First of all, I will identify the cause of underperformance. If the under-performers were dealing with a personal issue, I would align with them and show understanding. Then ask what the company can do for them, be it adjusting roles or increasing exposure to developers. I would come up with a schedule with them to evaluate if the changes help.

In other cases it might be a question of project fit. I would reevaluate the allocation of the tasks and adjust them if needed. Providing the right training or upskilling could also be an option.

Q5. How do you inspire / work well with others?

Aim of the question: To evaluate your leadership and collaboration ability.

Strategy:

✓ Show that you can maintain healthy relationships in the workplace.

✓ Mention how focusing the user should engage and bring people together.

✓ Taking initiative to brainstorm or share insights.

✗ Having little interest in collaborating with others.

✓ Example

I have a collaborative spirit, willing and eager to work with others toward the same goals. I will frequently brainstorm with the team to come up with the best quality work. I find talking to our users exciting. Therefore I will also work closely with the users and other teams throughout the project, making sure we share ideas and insight. I believe that driving for quality and having a goal to form a world-class team can inspire my teammates and increase engagement.

Q6. What motivates you as a manager?

Aim of the question: To evaluate your resiliency and determination to fulfill the need for this role.

Strategy:

✓ Show them you care more than the paycheck, be energetic and enthusiastic.

✓ Valid understanding of what makes a good manager, for example: understanding people and motivating a team.

✗ Lack of interest in managing a good team or problem-solving.

✓ Example

I am a curious person who wants to solve customer issues by design. As I have gained experience I have enjoyed playing a more leading role in order to take the initiative in tasks like motivating a team to solve problems. I am also very motivated by understanding each team members' strengths and helping them succeed.

Q7. What team culture would you like to establish?

Aim of the question: To estimate whether your management style would align with the company culture.

Strategy:

✓ Avoid simply answering the criteria a team is supposed to acquire, such as work jointly with each other, have effective communication, etc.

✓ Share your vision, this is a chance to show some of your thinking on how to lead.

✓ Be concrete. You need to provide a workable plan to support the answer.

✓ **Example**

I want to establish a team with a world-class design practice and bring quality results that make us proud. To do so, I will ensure the above intention is clear to each teammate. We, as a team, will pursue a growth mindset, focus on what we can become, and have the mindset that we can always be better.

To be more precise, I will build digital standards and guidelines which introduce the culture around consistency, best practices and improvement, and even tone of voice. I will also develop the habit to have weekly sharing meetings and regular social lunches or activities, allowing the team to learn and get used to sharing problems and knowledge.

Q8. What is your experience with stakeholder management?

Aim of the question: To assess whether you can coordinate with teams and other stakeholders.

Strategy:

✓ Use the SCAR technique.

✓ Show your problem-solving skills, such as prioritisation and being customer-oriented.

✓ Mention the method and result.

✓ **Example**

When I was working with the Customer Relations department and Global Call Centre at United Airlines, I managed different stakeholders by getting a common understanding of all the problems they had previously raised with work done by my department.

After this, I created a list, which acted as a source of truth of all the issues and kept it updated. Then my team and I worked through them based on how important they were and which ones were possible to fix with the resources we had. I organised meetings with relevant teams to try to understand and fix issues and reported any progress back to the stakeholders. Finally, this led to breakthrough fixes, as we had the data and customer insight to back up the changes we wanted to make.

Another example was my work on the airline booking management system. The new design did not test well with users, which indicated that a change in design was necessary.

Therefore, I organised meetings to convince different stakeholders, namely the Manage Booking Team, Business Analyst and Project designers. To be more convincing, I visualised the insights and data from the user tests so everyone could understand clearly. This later led to a change in the UX flow.

Personality & Future Development

Along with your qualifications, background and design experience, the recruiter needs to know your plans for the future to decide whether you meet the company's long-term development goals.

Q1. *Tell me about yourself / Describe your personality*

Aim of the question: To know more about your character and decide whether you are suitable to join the team.

Strategy:

✓ Ensure your answer is unique and dynamic.

✓ Be sincere, and stay positive.

✗ Oversharing.

> **✓ Example**
>
> I am a curious person who is motivated by challenges. I love to discover what challenges people have and then try to use design to solve these problems. I also make the most out of every opportunity. For example, when I went on the Japan exchange, I made the most out of it and managed to do an internship in Tokyo to further my experience there.

Q2. *What's your biggest weakness?*

Aim of the question: To know whether you have a healthy self-awareness and a growth mindset.

Strategy:

✓ Mention skills that aren't critical for the job

✓ Remember to talk about how you improve on or turn it into a positive personality.

✓ Be careful with your choice; don't choose a minor or "not weakness at all" kind of answer. It will backfire, and you look like you are lacking humility and self-reflection.

✓ Example

I was a person who focused on details, trying to perfect everything, for example, the transition and timing, all by myself. As a team leader, it became a weakness. Nowadays I deal with it by three methods. First, by accepting that perfect is the enemy of done. Second, by maintaining the standard and efficiency by writing guidelines for the team. Third, ensure the team cares as much as I do, and delegate the problem-solving tasks to them.

Q3. How do you deal with stress?

Aim of the question: To know how pressure affects your performance and how you handle it. It would help if you took this question as an opportunity to prove that you are productive and capable of managing stress.

Strategy:

✓ Provide examples.

✓ Talk about how pressure motivates you.

✓ Mention what you've learnt from working under pressure.

✕ I never get stressed.

✓ Example

There is good and bad stress. For example, there was stress from redesigning the Bank of America app within a tight schedule and integrating the new and complicated payment system into the app. I took the pressure as a motivation to focus and work diligently to get those tasks done. It trained my team and me the skills of time management and prioritisation.

Q4. How did you start as a designer?

Aim of the question: This question is just a background check. It is a valuable chance to show your enthusiasm for design.

Strategy:

✓ Be prepared, aim at telling a complete, winning story.

✓ Example

I was interested in Architecture, Engineering and Design; after exploring all of those options, I found product design was the most fascinating one as it would be a way to solve problems and impact many people.

I decided to study at Glasgow School of Art, as the course is run by a sociologist. It had a curriculum that really looked into understanding people.

Q5. What do you want to achieve in 3-5 years? / What are your long-term career goals?

Aim of the question: Your career goals are relevant to your recruiter. They want to hire someone self-motivated, proactive, a person who is likely to stick around and work hard.

Strategy:

✓ Don't be too specific. Every company has a unique promotion plan, and office culture, answering this question too specifically may raise doubts on whether you would be fit for the position. Tailoring the answer and aligning with your industry development instead of focusing too much on the role.

✓ Mention that you are aiming at a long-term career. Unless you are applying for a part-time or freelancing job, you should always show that you are ready to settle in and grow with the company.

✓ Demonstrate your passion and intention to expand beyond your skill set.

✗ Mention you want immediately be something unrelated to the role you are interviewing for.

✓ Example

First of all, I've worked on consumer-facing apps, with many successes. I've also worked on an app which serves the very forefront of the digital banking business. Hence my goal is to keep contributing to good design, solving new problems and face different challenges. Second, I hope to work with other thought leaders, innovators and lead a bigger team and more global team to achieve more.

Q6. Given your history, how long would you expect to stay in this role?

Aim of the question: It is a tricky question. Again, the recruiters tend to avoid people with short job stints because they want their investment to pay off.

Strategy:

✓ Let them know the role attracts you.

✓ Focus on contribution and achievement during your stay.

✓ Show that you understand the context, try to suggest a realistic period.

✓ **Example**

I usually let my contribution and satisfaction determine my employment period because I aim at bringing high value to every job role that I'm in.

For example, when I worked at Transit, I supported the company mapping from 8 cities to 27 cities. My contribution also helped it win the Paris Metro Competition and featured in one of the Apple Press Conferences.

With this role and the tough challenges come along, in addition to my goal to create and manage a design team which obtains progressive culture; I would say at least staying for a few years.

Q7. Tell me more about your experience working in this industry?

Aim of the question: Whether it is the fintech or health industry, the recruiters may be keen on knowing if you have experience in the same industry to the job you are interviewing for.

Strategy:

✓ Describe the experience that can connect to the position you apply for.

✓ Provide supporting facts on why you are qualified to take the job.

✓ If you don't have much experience, show that you are interested in the industry (for example the crowdfunding mentioned below) or have some related side project.

✓ **Example**

I have a substantial interest in the transformation of banks and financial institutions. I lead the UX team at the Bank of America, which worked on a digital wallet integrated with various payment infrastructures.

Outside of work, I have also taken part in the crowdfunding of Monzo Bank because I believe they will set a new standard moving ahead.

Q8. Tell me something that is not on your CV.

Aim of the question: To look for some extra factors that indicate whether you are suitable for the job.

Strategy:

✓ Share some strengths, achievements or side projects.

✓ Be strategic. Choose something that suggests you have other skills that can help you do the job.

✓ **Example**

I have participated in some other interesting projects at my previous work for Transit, such as working on features for the Apple Watch app, which was presented at the Apple Keynote behind Tim Cook!

I have also developed an app called Sessions. It can track activities and help users turn the preferable ones to habits. Tumblr's iOS app lead has recommended it and lifehack.org has chosen it as one of the Best Habit Tracking Apps in 2020.

Design insight

An ideal UX designer candidate should be a sharp-witted visionary. Therefore, besides asking questions about your design process, the recruiter may ask about your insight into the industry.

Q1. What does UX mean to you?

Aim of the question: To determine whether you really understand what UX is.

Strategy:

✓ Support the answer with personal opinions and perspective

✓ Show that you understand how UX fits in with the bigger picture

✓ Demonstrate how insightful and enthusiastic you are about the industry.

✓ **Example**

User Experience is really about the experience being greater than the sum of its parts. It integrates the brand, technology, functionality, usability, strategy and most importantly the user.

Our work is meaningful because it acknowledges the need to understand users to create excellent products. Our job represents the superb voice of the user that deserves to be listened to by understanding what is meaningful and what isn't. UX is best placed to do this. UX is not only important for designing features but also coming up with new ones and making an overall better product.

Q2. How do you simplify experiences?

Aim of the question: A user-centred design should be easy to understand and use. The recruiters are looking for someone who isn't going to list out all the features but will carefully think them through.

Strategy:

✓ Give a specific example of how you made a complex experience easy.

✓ Explain the process in how you did it and the result.

✕ Basic answer which doesn't give any detail.

✓ **Example**

When I worked on the transport app at Transit, I integrated Uber to the mix of public transport options. There was a lot of information to communicate: the arrival time, the transit time, the cost, the surcharge etc. I worked quickly on several different concepts and tested them with users to see which ones they understood the quickest.

It simplified the process for users who want to include Uber as one of the possible transit options in their journeys. I received good feedback at the time that it was easier to order an Uber via our app than the Uber app itself.

Q3. If I gave you a feature, how would you prioritise it?

Aim of the question: To see whether the company can count on you to get work done without someone standing over your shoulder.

Strategy:

✓ Be specific about how you manage your workload.

✓ As detailed and thorough as possible.

✕ Little or no thought into how to prioritise a feature.

✓ **Example**

If you gave me a feature request, I would first think it through, including whether it has the potential to help the company's KPI (key performance indicators) and whether it benefits the user. After ensuring the request is validated, the user stories can be so quickly prescriptive. The team may come up with other approaches or methods to achieve the same goal too.

I would also consider the product road map, The team would discuss whether there is anything upcoming that may make this easier. Speaking to the development teams would give us an estimate of how long it might take to build.

All tasks would be arranged based on their time, scope, quality, and resource; finally tasks can be based on the specialisms and capacities of the designers.

Q4. What motivates you as a designer?

Aim of the question: Convince the recruiter that you have resiliency and determination to fulfill the need for this role.

Strategy:

✓ Show them you care more than the paycheck, be energetic and enthusiastic.

✓ Show them that you are curious, are user focused and like solving problems.

✗ Lack of interest in designing.

✓ **Example**

I am passionate about different aspects of being a designer. I am a curious person who believes good design solves our problems and improves our lives. Therefore, working as a designer offers me the chance to do so. I can also create a better design by getting customer insight and taking care of their needs.

Q5. How do you stay on top of trends or track interesting developments in the industry?

Aim of the question: To see whether you have a growth mindset and be self-motivated.

Strategy:

Most employers want to hire employees who are forward-thinking and keep an eye on trends hitting their industry or outside. Therefore:

✓ Demonstrate that you are self-motivated and constantly acquiring insight that can help the company go beyond the status quo.

✓ I would recommend you indeed regularly spend time researching the latest trends, not just for this particular interview question. Your insight will be helpful throughout the interview.

✗ Saying that you are not interested either in chasing trends or other players in the industry or at all.

✓ **Example**

I do it in various ways. I listen to related podcasts, come across, read and save insightful articles in the pocket reader. I also watch Google IO and Apple Keynote to keep up the latest development. I follow some outstanding figures and big thinkers on social media to look out for ongoing discussions within the field.

Q6. Are there any new technologies or processes that have caught your attention recently?

Aim of the question: This question may come as a follow-up question after the previous one. Therefore you must walk the walk.

Strategy:

✓ Show that you have an interest in new developments and have a desire to stay relevant.

✓ Elaborate your answer by mentioning the reason it caught your attention and your effort to understand it.

✗ Name a few technologies without further explanation.

✓ Example

Yes, there are a few! I am trying out some new designing tools and learning to code in Swift. The development of cryptocurrency also caught my eyes. For example, I am following the news and innovation related to digital wallets.

Q7. Name your favourite apps, or those that offer a great user experience.

Aim of the question: This can be a fun question but it can throw you off, so make sure you prepare a good answer. The objective of this question is to know more about your thinking process and your understanding of user experience.

Strategy:

✓ Specify a particular feature or example from a product.

✓ Elaborate on the reasons and deliver constructive comments.

✗ Little or no idea how to answer it.

✓ Example

I think Airbnb has a decent design. It is consistent with its service. It provides the feeling of home with the help of colours, language and white space in the app. Besides, the designers organise the content well so the users can easily find what they need.

Another example is the app Transit. Although it might be a little biased for me to say so, I enjoy using this app. It has some fantastic functions and users can easily look for travel times, correct exits and the next carriage. It is also extremely relatable, as it uses 'casual' language which is part of its own tone of voice.

Employment details

Hold on. Stay sharp. It's almost finished. When the following questions appear, it usually suggests the interview is going to end soon.

Q1. Do you have any questions for us?

Aim of the question: To clarify any doubts the candidates have and see how engaging they are. Some people want the interview to end ASAP and say a quick no. Remember, always say YES.

Strategy:

✓ Be engaging. Show that you are interested in the position by asking questions about the project, career path or current challenges.

✓ Be prepared and have an agile mind. Prepare three to five questions to ask, and it would be better if you can touch on topics related to anything mentioned in the interview.

✗ Say no / I think you covered everything I wanted to know. I'm sure I'll have more questions if I get the job.

✓ Example

What is the current team structure?
What are the biggest challenges someone would face in this role?
Why should I join the company and specifically this role?
What is the most exciting part of this role?

Q2. What is your notice period?

The shorter notice period you offer, the higher chance you get hired. If your notice period is long, provide options to shorten it. For example to buy out, or use your holiday. Only make the move if you are in a situation where you do want the job and the notice period is the problem.

Q3. What is your expected salary?

Questions about salary are always tricky. You know they have a budget. If your expected salary is too high, you may lose the opportunity; if it is lower than their budget, they probably will go along. To make things worse, they may consider it as an indicator that you are lacking experience and capability.

Research in the salary range for the position. This will help you understand where you sit, how aggressive to be and give you confidence to negotiate. Try not to reveal your current salary. If they do not make an offer first, just answer with what you expect. Only accept it if it is reasonable to the current market rate and proportional to the discussed responsibilities and your skillset.

CONCLUSION

Since I started my career, I'm lucky enough to have been able to have experience in different size and stage companies in different countries. To me, making great products with a strong focus on users and insight is fulfilling. Sharing my experiences with others has also been fulfilling and I really do recommend you do the same as a way of improving your soft skills and network.

This book is an amalgamation of my successes and failures, my research and my notes and countless months of editing. It is self-published and a project in itself. I do not make much from the book but believe it will be useful for others. If you believe this book has helped you in any way, please take a few moments to write a review of it on Amazon. It would really mean a lot to me.

Lastly, I'd like to say that I believe the industry will continue to grow by us pushing the boundaries, designing thoughtful products and showing that design adds value. Being a designer is not easy, so I hope you do keep trying and raise the profile of design, wherever it may be. I hope after reading this guide, you are now ready to take the next step. Hope you own the next interview and best of luck!

-Duane Harrison

Hong Kong